GW00854393

THE THISTLE AND THE ROSE

Arthur Gordon

Dear Jacky,

Sincere best wishes,

'Arthur Gordon'

ARTHUR H. STOCKWELL LTD
Torrs Park, Ilfracombe, Devon, EX34 8BA
Established 1898
www.ahstockwell.co.uk

British Library Cataloguing-in-Publication Data.
A catalogue record for this book is available
from the British Library.

ISBN 978-0-7223-4962-5
Printed in Great Britain by
Arthur H. Stockwell Ltd
Torrs Park   Ilfracombe
Devon EX34 8BA

CONTENTS

Foreword	5
The *Alexandra*	7
Kernow Bys Vykken (Cornwall Forever)	10
Berry Head	12
The Bikers	14
The Braemar Games	16
The Ceilidh	18
The Old Coach House	20
Autumn Leaves	22
The Mallock Clock Tower	23
Dartmoor	24
A Cruise Ship	26
The Duke of Buckleaux	27
The Falcons	28
Granny Agnes	30
Edinburgh	32
Game Birds	33
Hercules	34
The Messiah	36
Mind Yer Heed on the Lobby Gas	38
A Meeting	39
The Monster	40
The Opportunist	41
"Order, Order"	42
Paignton Pier	44
Grinding Poverty	45
A Ramble	46
A Robin	47
The Rowers	48
The Sea	49
The Seahorse	50
At the Seaside	51
The Storyteller	52
Sparrows and Chaffinches	54
Suburbia	55

Torquay   56

The Dragonfly and the Trout   58

A Tuna   60

A Song Thrush   62

Witches   63

The Wren   64

FOREWORD

This is my very first collection of poetry and I am delighted that Arthur H. Stockwell Ltd has kindly offered publication. My work covers an extensive range of subjects from my childhood in Scotland to later years in London and the West Country. Ultimately, themes of the West Country provide my main source of inspiration. The title, *The Thistle and the Rose* was an obvious choice. I was born in Scotland but I have lived most of my life in the West Country in England.

I particularly like to describe real places in my writing so that readers gain a true sense of the places of interest. Hopefully, they can imagine being at the actual place. For example, 'The Clock Tower' is about the Mallock Clock Tower, a real building at the harbourside in Torquay. Similarly for my other poems, such as 'Paignton Pier', 'Berry Head', 'Dartmoor' and 'Edinburgh'.

Also, I enjoy employing the skill of telling a story in poetic form. I feel that this is far more interesting and engaging for the reader than simply telling a tale. This influence is reflected in poems such as 'The Storyteller', 'Granny Agnes' and 'The *Alexandra*'.

I spent my youth in Scotland, and here in my poetry I have very much tried to introduce a true Scottish flavour. An interesting poem on this is 'Mind Yer Heed on the Lobby Gas'. I wrote this in traditional Scottish style and the title phrase is always a favourite in our house when guests are leaving.

Much of my work of course reflects the West Country. I live

in South Devon and I draw inspiration from a wide variety of sources: the countryside, the cliffs and seashores, the flora and fauna and local heritage. I enjoy writing about the rugged Devon coast, the wild cliffs, sheltered beaches and marine life that thrives in the coastal waters. I suppose that one of the main reasons I write about the West Country is that, along with many people, I like to celebrate and share with others the simple beauty to be enjoyed in this part of the world.

My writing is meant to be interesting and thoughtful and, most importantly, I sincerely hope that readers simply enjoy the pleasure of my endeavours.

Finally, I must of course express my gratitude to all of the staff at Arthur H. Stockwell Ltd for their help and assistance.

Arthur Gordon, 11 February 2019

THE *ALEXANDRA*

Now gather round, friends and family,
For I have a salty tale to tell,
Of my travels abroad at sea –
Plenty of time before our host rings the old brass bell.
I was press-ganged in the town of Ilfracombe
And taken to the *Alexandra* in Bristol,
A mighty tall ship at the quayside.
They put me aboard and furnished me with sword and pistol.

A few days later, with crew on board,
We slipped anchor on the morning tide –
An adventure at sea was beginning.
I was mighty scared, I do confide.
The *Alexandra* sailed out of the Bristol Channel –
Soon we were out of sight of land.
The sails were full and the sea was calm,
Seagulls followed us and the weather was grand.

The *Alexandra* ploughed on in the sea swell.
We were led by Captain Edward McKay, a kindly Scot –
He steadied the ship at the helm.
As to his plans, he did not say a lot.
Soon we were sailing off the coast of Cornwall;
We made progress in the wild open sea.
With a westerly breeze we made good time –
The sound of the wind in the rigging did not bother me.

As we sailed on a vicious storm brewed.
Soon we were crossing the Bay of Biscay.
Waves as high as a house lashed the decks –
We made it through with a few drams of whisky.
Throughout this heavy weather
The crew continued to tack and beat.
The work was hard, the hours long;
It was good to rest my aching feet.

At night under a star-filled sky,
The *Alexandra* creaked and groaned.
Often thrown from their bunks,
The crew scowled and moaned.
The ship was old, but handled well –
The steady Captain McKay continued to steer.
One fine day I stood on deck –
I could see the Straits of Gibraltar draw near.

The Captain said we would stop in Gibraltar,
For the resupply of fresh water and food.
The crew swigged their daily tot of dark rum –
The thought of staying in port improved their mood.
Now the ship duly docked in the port of Gibraltar;
The crew went ashore – there was lots to see and do.
None of the crew spoke Spanish.
We must have looked a ragged, motley crew.

After three days' rest the *Alexandra* set sail again.
Captain McKay rose to speak and raised his hand.
He said we were a slave ship Morocco-bound –
The tip of Africa, a diverse and strange land.
Soon we arrived in Morocco,
A heavily populated bustling port –
Spaniards, French, Arabs and Africans together –
Guarded by an ancient fortified fort.

The crew and I accompanied Captain McKay ashore.
There were 120 souls in chains on the quay.
They looked poorly fed and miserable –
A life of slavery was their destiny.
Soon the auction got under way –
Captain McKay bought most of the slaves.
The crew felt sorry for them –
They would end up in early graves.

The slaves were taken on board,
And to the lower decks beneath.
They were given a hearty soup,
And the ship's doctor checked their teeth.
Then I reminded Captain McKay
Of a cargo we had forgotten.
I knew the Captain had orders
To buy bales of the finest Egyptian sheets of cotton.

Duly laden, the *Alexandra* set sail.
Homeward-bound, we ate our hot stew.
As to our further adventures together,
The crew debated, but none of them really knew.
On the way back the weather was kind –
The Bay of Biscay was like a pond.
I had come to love the *Alexandra*,
And of the ship's crew I was very fond.

After two weeks at sea we returned to Bristol –
The wretched slaves had been caught.
Wealthy merchants arrived to view them;
For a life of drudgery and work they were bought.
I then said goodbye to Captain McKay and crew –
A maritime life was not for me.
Life at sea was tough and cruel;
I wanted to see my family, share a joke and drink tea.

KERNOW BYS VYKKEN
(CORNWALL FOREVER)

The Grand Bard of Gorsedh Kernow,
She wears a blue frock right down to her shoes.
The Bard is the head of Kernow;
She is both writer, poet and muse.

The Bard and colleagues in blue frocks
Have an important mission:
To encourage the Cornish language.
It is part of their tradition.

They meet for various ceremonies,
Their status, the 'Cornish National Minority'.
Their language originates in Celtic.
Its promotion is their priority.

Cornwall is a long peninsula – in the far west, Land's End.
It is a very rural, with rolling hills of farmland,
A rugged coastline, surrounded by the sea.
Kernow has many beaches of golden sand.

Kernow is the home of the Cornish folk,
Farming the main occupation, with cattle and sheep.
In upland areas, like Bodmin Moor,
The land is bog and marsh, the hills steep.

Kernow has a past history
For the mining of tin and lead.
These industries have passed their time;
Now they cater for tourists instead.

In Cornwall there are lots of coves,
And wide beaches like Carlyon Bay,
Ideal for boating and surfers.
In summer, sailors come to stay.

From Bude and Padstow in the north, down to Camborne,
Falmouth, Penzance and St Ives,
The Grand Bard and friends
Ensure the Cornish language survives.

BERRY HEAD

In South Devon there lies an area of natural beauty
Known as Berry Head.
The cliffs there are probably the highest in England,
The local folk say, or so it is said.

Upon Berry Head there is mounted a lighthouse.
It is painted once a year, pure white.
The lighthouse is the shortest in Britain;
In the dark, its flashing light is very bright.

Seabirds nest on the rocky cliffs –
Common birds such as gulls, gannets and shags.
The shags dry their outstretched wings,
Perched on the rocky crags.

On the bare cliffs and scrub,
Seabirds gather in flocks.
They patrol the open seas,
And make nests in the grey rocks.

In the cloudless summer sky
Herring gulls glide, majestic in flight.
They catch fry for their chicks,
Who always squabble and fight.

Gannets and gulls are in large numbers.
They circle in the sky, then dive,
Grasping fish in their gullets.
The sea is their home and they thrive.

On the coast at Berry Head
The sea is always choppy and rough.
To the seabirds this is of no matter –
They are very hardy and tough.

THE BIKERS

"Make way, make way!"
There is a roar from the bikes as they drive.
"I say, I say, I say."
Along the seafront, in packs, the bikers arrive.

They gather in droves on the seafront.
They can ride at a fair pace.
Although they are friends,
Sometimes they like to race.

There are various machines on display –
Triumph, Yamaha and Harley Davidson bikes.
Some have three wheels –
They call them trikes.

Now the bikers have badges on their leathers;
Some are quite obviously crude.
Across their petrol tanks
They have a naughty nude.

Whilst in Paignton they visit the Spinning Wheel –
They like to have a beer, a good drink.
Keep away from the sea, lads.
If you fall in, you'll sink!

Now the local traffic warden,
At least he has some sense.
He stays away from bikers –
He's not that dense.

I stop to admire a motorbike;
The owner says "It's a BMW.
If you don't touch it,
I won't trouble you."

They wear heavy black leathers
And pieces of chain mail.
Some look quite tough;
No doubt, a few have been in jail.

I know about motorbikes – I read *MCN*,
I have a mate who is a 'Satan Slave'.
His real name is Peregrine Marmaduke Quilter,
But everyone calls him Dave.

I live near Paignton Pier,
And from my little home
I can see all the motorbikes –
Thick leather seats and brightly polished chrome.

There are thousands of bikes on the seafront –
The BMAD boys are back in town.
BMAD – bikers make a difference –
Try not to mow everyone down.

THE BRAEMAR GAMES

In the north of Scotland lies Braemar,
Where folks gather to attend
The famous Highland Games.
Once a year, a day they will spend,
Lads and lassies and wee bairns.
Friends and neighbours meet at Braemar –
They come to spectate or take part,
And arrive on foot, bicycle or by car.

Her Majesty the Queen and the royals
Lend dignity to the occasion.
As they arrive in the royal cars,
The crowd gives them a standing ovation.
The massed band gathers;
They then do the march past,
Playing 'God Save the Queen'.
The Highland Games can begin at last.

Folks come from far and wide –
Aberdeen, Stirling, Edinburgh and Leith.
They travel the lengthy miles
Across moorland and craggy heath.
Driving on lonely Scots roads,
They gradually make their way,
Picnic hampers in the boot
To see them through the endless day.

The athletes warm up for the cross-country run,
Up the brae and along the glen,
Over the old bridge and the dusty track.
Everyone wonders who will be first, ye ken.
Meanwhile men in their tartan kilts,
The caber they prepare to lift and toss.
They wipe their brows in the heat,
And will show the caber who is boss.

On the wooden stage the dancers swirl,
They hoot, yell and clap their hands
As they move in rhythm
To the sound of the Highland bands.
The pipers from the Black Watch
Make a deafening sound;
At the back, the drummers beat
And tap their feet upon the ground.
As the music plays and the athletes compete,
The youngsters paddle in the wee burn.
They remove their shoes and socks.
The stream is narrow, so they each take a turn –
It is a hot summer's day.
In the tent folks drink their beer,
They meet and tell yarns,
And so ends another year.

THE CEILIDH

Couples gathered at the kirk hall –
They were all there to have a ball.
Musicians formed upon the stage –
The Highland fling was all the rage.

Storytellers came from far and wide –
They came from the islands, on the boats McBride.
They told their Scottish yarns and tales,
And blethered as they quaffed the Scots-brewed ales.

Tartans of every possible hue –
Cameron, Stuart and Murray too.
Tartan, kilt, sporran and dirk
Were all on display at the kirk.

Ladies in their sparkling tartan dresses
Longed for their partners' caresses.
Lads and lassies danced with glee,
Together, young or old and free.

They clicked and tapped their heels
To the sound of the Highland reels,
Dancers in their tartan fashion,
Moving with unrivalled passion.

Hornpipe, reel and jig
Were all performed at the gig.
They would dance till the dewy dawn,
And see in the early morn.

Jig or reel, they waited for the piper's call.
They knew them well – they knew them all.
The ladies' dresses swished and swirled,
Sweet faces smiling and their hair curled.

Girls and boys exchanged a glance –
Who would pick them for a dance?
Dance with me, if you please.
I move with style and with ease.

They came from Arbroath and Ardrossan –
None had ever been forgotten.
They danced and reeled with panache and style,
Then they rested for a wee while.

The music was a thrill for all,
Whether young or old, short or tall.
Everyone had their favourite move –
They sure knew how to hit that groove.

Firstly a hornpipe, then a jig.
"Hi. My name's Maisie. I'm from Bonnyrigg."
"Oh, that's very nice. My name is Paul.
I was born in County Donegal."

And as the pipers blew and blew,
Louder and louder the music grew.
There was no rest for any at all –
This was the ceilidh, this was the ball.

THE OLD COACH HOUSE

The Old Coach House is a traditional Devonian pub,
Near Paignton Parish Church and Palace Place Social Club.
The landlord and staff welcome customers with a smile.
They are content for visitors to stay a while.

At the entrance there is a sign,
Which has been there a very long time:
'There are no strangers in here,
Just friends who have not yet met.'
Customers talk at the wooden bar –
Regulars come from near and far.

By the fire lies an old sheepdog;
Outside the weather is misty with slight fog.
In winter the fire glows;
In the overcast sky the wind blows.

The pub has central pillars of stone and brick,
On the ceiling the black oak beams are solid and thick.
The walls are made up of mud and wattle,
And real ale is sold by the glass or the bottle.

The Coach House has oak tables and seats –
Family and friends gather and meet.
A young man with a girl has a natter –
A pretty girl the man wishes to flatter.

The regulars are of good cheer –
Some have been going there for many a year.
Couples talk on their first date.
The pub stays open until quite late.

By the hearth in the gloom,
There stands a witch with a broom.
She is fully dressed with a black witch's pointed hat,
The only thing missing, her trusty black cat.

There are signs on the wall, a coach to Bristol.
In those days coachmen carried a sword and a pistol.
Travellers could catch a coach and horses to Penzance,
Or to London, then by boat to France.

'Stage Fare,
Paignton to London,
One Shilling and Nine Pence, Three Farthings.'

'Stage Fare,
Paignton to Penzance
One Shilling and a Penny Ha'penny.'

'Stage Fare,
Paignton to Bristowe,
One Shilling and Three Pence.'

On Fridays musicians sing their songs;
Folks listen in their throngs.
Customers enjoy their stay,
Then homeward-bound make their way.

AUTUMN LEAVES

The winter solstice has begun.
It is a time on the farm for hearty work and toil.
The tractor and plough take to the land
To plough and prepare the rich red soil.

On the flat plain of the Exe Valley,
Winter wheat and barley are sown.
Crows gather to feast on the planted seed.
In spring the grain will be ripe and full-grown.

Wintry rain scours the bare ploughed land;
Fallen, dry leaves turn and tap the ground.
Dusk soon ends the overcast short days,
The nocturnal call of a nightjar the only sound.

In the nearby villages and towns,
In the cheerless grey and coming of the night,
The birds roost early in the trees.
Street lamps come on early, yellow and bright.

Boats head for the safety of the harbour,
With the onset of autumn rain and gales,
Mariners come ashore to a welcome inn,
Yachtsmen moor their boats and furl their sails.

The West Country rivers swell with wintry rain –
The flowers will bloom in spring again.
On the seashore the wind rises and the waters seethe.
This is the season of autumn leaves.

THE MALLOCK CLOCK TOWER

By Torquay Harbour sits the Mallock clock tower,
A Victorian monument of sandstone.
In the middle of a busy road
It stands erect and alone.

The tower has been recently cleaned.
It stands about 100 feet high.
Busy shoppers hardly notice it
As they pass or scurry by.

Close by the harbour and the moored-up boats,
The clock tower is part of our heritage and history.
Nearby, Vaughan Parade and the local shops.
How long it has been there is a total mystery.

It is worth saying,
The clock tower has a lovely Westminster chime.
If you stand and view it,
You can always tell the time.

DARTMOOR

In the centre of Devon is an upland –
A lonely place called Dartmoor.
The landscape is wild and hilly,
And the soil is generally poor.

There are many hamlets and villages –
Chagford, Lustleigh, Widecombe in the Moor and Poundsgate.
Sturdy houses, often built from cob,
The roofs are thatch or local slate.

The land can be bare, mainly rough grass and gorse.
There are tors on the hilltops –
Hare Tor, Kitty Tor, Rippon Tor and Haytor.
The tors are bleak rocky outcrops.

In the sheltered woodland valleys
There is many an isolated farm and homestead.
They tend sheep and cattle;
In their Devon longhouses they bake their own bread.

Dartmoor is a damp place with heavy rain;
For many of Devon's rivers it is the source.
The Rivers Tavy, Taw, Dart and Teign,
From Dartmoor they flow and run their course.

In the lowland lush meadows
There are flocks of black-faced sheep.
They graze and ramble in the grass;
In the spring their lambs jump and leap.

In nearby fields, walled in by stone,
Cattle quietly chew the cud.
Cows with calves by their side,
Their hooves sink deep in the dark mud.

Livestock graze the pastures
And tramp across the moorland heather.
Buzzards patrol the endless skies.
Often there is inclement weather.

Local folks warm their hands
At home or in the pub by the fire,
While outside the rain pours down,
Filling the bogs and mire.

Groups of walkers stop for a rest –
Dartmoor can be icy-cold.
They visit the Warren House Inn or the Rock at Haytor –
The pubs are mainly thatched and very old.

In the cattle and hay barns
Farmers feed the chickens and fowl.
The birds scratch in the hay and earth,
Watched overhead by a solitary barn owl.

On the scraggy moorland heather
Live small herds of Dartmoor ponies.
They have thick coats and rugged manes,
Fed by passing tourists and their cronies.

Visitors can find the going tough –
The moorland can be very steep,
With narrow winding footpaths.
The land is best suited to sheep.

A CRUISE SHIP

I could see in the water
A cruise ship in Torbay.
Swaying in the breeze, at anchor,
It had come for a brief stay.

Sunlight dancing on the ship's hull,
Whilst the ship was in dock
The tourists disembarked to view
The sights of 'London Bridge' and Thatcher Rock.

The seamen man the vast decks,
As crew they dress in white.
They stroll the wooden decks on duty –
To the ladies they make a handsome sight.

On their days of rest
The seamen have a run ashore.
In their finest civvies,
Into the local pubs they will pour.

The passengers are of every profession –
Teachers, tailors and engineers,
They chat in the bars together
As they drink their ice-cold beers.

In rota they dine at high table.
The Captain toasts with a glass of wine.
"Welcome aboard –
The pleasure is all mine."

With cries of "Hoist the anchor,"
The ship stayed just a few days.
The seamen had their sailing orders –
The ship steamed away in the morning haze.

THE DUKE OF BUCKLEAUX

"The Duke of Buckleaux,
That's who."
"Who? The Duke of Buckleaux?"
"I've already said that's who."
"Who and what is the Duke of Buckleaux?"
"I am the Duke of Buckleaux. How do you do?"
"Long live the Duke of Buckleaux."

Now I'm frae Scotland if ye ken,
And I've now finished with ma wee pen.
If you like my poems I canny tell;
Nevertheless I wish ye well.

THE FALCONS

A pair of peregrine falcons live
In an eyrie near the beach.
It's built into the cliff –
There is plenty of prey within easy reach.

The falcons roam the cliffs and sea;
Their plumage is a silvery blue.
Their talons are as hard as steel;
Their feathers have a beruffled hue.

Their calls sound like 'Kia, kia',
With eyes sharp and bright.
Male and female are a loving pair,
And can see very well at night.

As for the falcons' diet,
They often dine on wood pigeon,
Or if they have good fortune,
Perhaps even a nice fresh widgeon.

At the falcon's dining table,
The remains of a pigeon can often be seen,
Near its clifftop nest,
The wings untouched, the breast picked clean.

The pair search for prey,
And fly with consummate ease,
Launching from their clifftop home
In the refreshing sea breeze.

Now in their woody nest
The falcon pair have kin.
They have duly mated –
Two downy chicks live within.

The pair are always busy –
Two chicks they have to feed.
They hunt from dawn to dusk
To satisfy their constant greed.

The pair take it in turns to patrol the skies,
With awesome skill,
Searching for prey;
They can easily make a strike and kill.

GRANNY AGNES

Granny was a lovely old lady.
She would say, "Och, ma wee hen."
She lived with us for many a year.
I dinny know what it means, ye ken.

"See the wee chukie birdies."
She referred to the sparrows in the trees.
She spoke as she strolled on the lawn
In the cool afternoon breeze.

During her married life
She had three wains –
Three lovely wee daughters,
Who grew into beautiful bairns.

Agnes was proud of her kin –
A bevvy of young girls.
She doted on them all the time.
One had straight hair; the other two, curls.

Agnes was born in Scotland;
Her husband, Arthur, made watches and clocks.
As she grew older her sight waned,
And Arthur often wore odd socks.

When Arthur passed away,
Granny was in an offy plight.
She sold their flat in Stirling –
To her daughter in Perth she took flight.

The daughter, Netty, in Perth,
Could be a cantankerous wee tyke.
Agnes and Netty lived in a croft by the loch –
There were many people Netty did not like.

Now Agnes and Netty
Were not the only two in the croft;
Other residents also lived there –
House martins in the eaves and bats in the loft.

Agnes lived in a retirement home –
She reached the great age of ninety-seven.
She was looked after very well,
Then God took her into care – she went to heaven.

EDINBURGH

Edinburgh has both a castle and a palace –
It is an enchanting city.
With the Princes Gardens and many parks,
It is truly very pretty.

Just outside the city
Lies the famous Arthur's Seat –
An old volcanic hilltop,
Where lovers like to meet.

With Holyrood Palace
And the Royal Mile,
Tourists who visit
Like to sightsee a while.

There are places like Musselburgh and Leith –
They sit astride the estuary, the Firth of Forth,
The waters traversed by the Forth Bridge.
The meandering river runs its course.

Princes Street is well known for its many pubs –
A pub crawl there is a task indeed.
As you call at every hostelry,
You need stamina to succeed.

Then there is the famous Edinburgh Tattoo.
At the end, the piper plays on the castle battlement;
The spectators listen in awe
As the piper plays a Scottish lament.

In the distance the Pentland Hills –
Dark clouds often gather and rumble.
The hills are deep blue in colour –
Soon again the rains will tumble.

GAME BIRDS

The grouse is plump and of medium size,
It has feathered legs and small eyes,
It lives on the open moor,
It feeds on the heather, its diet is poor.

The little partridge generally lives on open ground,
It weighs no more than about a pound,
It likes to eat seed and grain,
It has a vegetarian diet in the main.

Now, the pheasant resides in fields and hedges,
It lives on various seeds and sedges.
The male is very blue in colour;
The female's plumage is much duller.

The mallard and the widgeon are our most common duck,
Their feathers they like to groom and pluck.
They paddle easily on rivers and streams.
Weeds seem to be their diet – they like their greens.

With such beautiful birds,
To hunt them for sport is absurd.
It is almost obscene
To shoot them and pick their bones clean.

HERCULES

Hercules lies near the railway line,
In a siding, quietly at rest,
Gathering its mighty strength
For tomorrow, to give its best.

Daily it carries a heavy load,
Thundering down the well-worn railway track,
Taking passengers from Paignton to Kingswear
Via the banks of the River Dart, and then back.

Hercules is a triumph of engineering –
It has enormous mechanical powers.
Fuelled by water and coal,
Over man and beast it towers.

The footman on the footplate supplies coal –
Into the boiler it rapidly burns.
The driver and footman work tirelessly –
To shovel coal they each take turns.

Working at the footplate,
The team daily toil
To supply fuel and water for the engine
In the intense heat, grime and oil.

Hercules is admired by many –
A testament to Victorian skill.
For train enthusiasts and visitors,
It provides them all with a thrill.

As it works up a head of steam,
To depart the railway station,
Passengers click their cameras
And give it a standing ovation.

Passengers who board the Victorian carriages,
Then gaze out the windows of the train
At the gently flowing River Dart
And the passing woods and fields of ripening grain.

Across the viaduct designed by Mr I. K. Brunel,
The suns glints on *Hercules*' metal body and funnel.
The driver toots the whistle twice
As the train chugs into the old brick-built tunnel.

As *Hercules* steams around the bend,
Onlookers say, "Look – here it comes."
A giant of iron and steel,
And weighing umpteen tonnes.

THE MESSIAH

Jesus Christ was the greatest One,
Prophet and Priest, God's only Son.
Amongst mortal men He was our King.
He taught the world to laugh and sing.

By God the Almighty He was appointed;
Disciples with water ensured He was anointed.
Jesus was more than just a Teacher;
He was God's chosen Preacher.

Jesus talked to mankind without prejudice or fear –
To God, every soul is precious and dear.
Jesus spoke to the world loud and clear,
Even when His own end was near.

God watched Jesus from the skies –
The Son of God never told lies.
He lived a life of beauty and grace;
He loved everyone of the human race.

Jesus was part of our creation,
Of every person in every nation.
He had boundless wit and charms,
And welcomed all of us in His arms.

God created the earth and seas,
To see mankind live well, free from disease.
With a happy and heartfelt song,
Man will live, bold and strong.

Summer sun, spring rain and winter snow –
Enjoy the evening and the sunset glow.
Life is a wonder and a celebration –
Enjoy the riches of God's Creation.

With His disciples, they had broken bread;
His followers anointed His head,
Washed His clothes and feet,
And wiped the dust off His shoes from the street.

In the end, the Son of God wore thorns for a crown.
He died for this world – He never let anyone down.
He told of God's love,
In every city, village and town.

Christ passed away on the Cross –
By far this world's greatest loss.
To the world He had told His story –
Jesus went to heaven and everlasting glory.

Soli Deo Gloria.
To God alone be glory.

MIND YER HEED ON THE LOBBY GAS

"Och, hello. Welcome in.
How's yer kith and kin?"
"I'm nay sure if they're well.
I have nay seen 'em. I canny tell."

"How's your son, the big yin?"
"I dinny know. When I called, he was nay in."
"The bonnie lassie next door has had a bairn."
"Och, I know her – she comes frae Nairn."

"You'll be having a wee dram with some ice?"
"That would be offy nice."
"I'll fill yer glass – just say when."
"You know me, ye ken."

"Drink it down afore ye go –
A lovely taste, you know.
Now, down the hall; as you pass,
Mind yer heed on the lobby gas."

"Aye."

A MEETING

The tiger watched the herd of zebra.
It began to stalk in the grass with stealth, keeping low.
The hot sweltering day was coming to an end –
The sun began to set with a fiery red glow.

The tiger moved close to a zebra on the edge of the herd.
"Hello, Mr Tiger," said the zebra.
"I was unaware that you were there."
"Oh," replied the tiger, "I was just passing
This busy thoroughfare."

The tiger crouched quietly.
"So, what do you want with me?"
The tiger cautiously replied,
"Well, I thought I may have you for my tea."

The zebra continued to munch the grass.
"But me you cannot devour –
I have a young foal
And I am a delicate flower."

"In addition," said the zebra,
"We are closely related." The zebra cried,
"We both have black stripes –
Your appetite will have to go unsatisfied."

"But you are wrong – I am a predator.
I am a hungry carnivore."
"Precisely," said the zebra. "We are related –
I am a four-legged herbivore."

The two moved together on the grassy plain.
"Thank you," said the tiger. "Now I see."
The zebra nodded towards the tiger.
"Would you like to stay for tea?"

THE MONSTER

In the salty sea below
There are creatures of many sizes.
There exist many a foe,
And also many surprises.

In the watery depths
Lurks the slimy, fickle conger eel.
With enormous jaws and teeth,
They are far from genteel.

Sheltered from storms above the sea,
The conger lives in the dark,
In the calmness of the gloom,
In wrecks like the *Cutty Sark*.

Its grey sleekit skin is silky smooth –
It likes to twist and slither.
In the dark shadows
It moves hither and thither.

The conger eel is just like Scotland –
Very long and thin.
If you knock upon his door,
You'll be very welcome in!

The conger has something of an appetite –
Any little morsel for tea,
A small snack or just a bite.
It could be you, it could be me!

You will be very sorry
If you try to catch him by rod and reel.
He has a canny eye,
And will see your boat's keel.

THE OPPORTUNIST

If you stroll along Paignton Seafront,
Grazing on the freshly cut green,
A group of fine donkeys
Will often be seen.

There are usually five animals,
Named Nosey, Paddy, Jack, Ben and Rockey.
Children pay a small price,
And ride them just like a jockey.

An opportunist crow watches from a fence.
The donkeys quietly feed on hay,
Swishing flies with their tails,
Some buckets of pony nuts not far away.

The crow squawks and stretches his wings –
His dark feathers have a soft, silky sheen.
With a long, sharp bill,
He gives his feathers a daily preen.

As the donkeys are distracted by the hay,
The crow flies to the top of the beach huts.
He peers down below
At a nearby bucket of pony nuts.

The crow swoops down to brim of the bucket,
And dips in his long black bill.
Up and down he dips and rises,
Until gradually he has had his fill.

"ORDER, ORDER"

"Order, order," the Speaker cries to the House.
The politicians holler and yell.
It is unfolding drama
As they give each other hell.

Politicians rise from their green leather seats
As they get ready to give their patter.
In their blue pinstripe suits
They address their chosen subject matter.

Parliamentary papers always at hand,
Unemployment or immigration,
Waving papers at the Opposition,
There is plenty of scope for their oration.

The Speaker follows the agenda;
The House then debates
A tedious subject, but of importance –
Tax increases and tax rebates.

They stand to speak; there is a quiet hush.
The MPs deliver their chosen speech;
Colleagues say, "Hear! hear!"
A glass of whisky within easy reach.

The Chancellor delivers his speech:
Excise duty on spirits and beer.
Pause for thought –
These go up again in the coming year.

So similarly for other goods,
Tobacco and cigars,
Plus a little extra –
A tax increase on cars.

And that's not all –
I haven't finished yet –
A duty increase too
For those who like to bet.

PAIGNTON PIER

A remnant of the Victorian era,
Protruding into the sea sits Paignton Pier.
A monolith of wood and steel,
It has survived for many a year.

They used to produce the 'End of the Pier Show',
Especially at Christmas, a pantomime.
Afterwards, the thespians' party –
"Oh, darling, you were simply divine."

The actors and actresses perform elsewhere –
Sadly, the shows are no more.
It is the age of the gaming and slot machine,
The only sound now, the waves lapping the shore.

The thespians provided tourist entertainment.
They told jokes and sang bawdy songs.
They performed sketches and dances –
Folks came in their throngs.

When you stroll along the pier,
Some of the sun-dried boards are warped and creak.
Selected areas are always cordoned off –
The wooden structure is quite weak.

Local people say that
Torbay Council should connive
To use their power
To keep the End of the Pier Show alive.

GRINDING POVERTY

I walked the narrow street;
A mother openly weeps.
"My darlings, the cupboard is bare.
I have no job or money.
I love you, my children.
I will do my best –
That is only proper for you.
I know you love me,
And I love you too."

A RAMBLE

I passed the pub, The Manor Inn;
I could hear the banter and the natter.
With fine ale in full swing,
They love to sit and chatter.

I continued along the country path,
Past the farm where they make cream.
The sun now low in the sky,
I walked along the banks of the stream.

I crossed a field with dewy grass,
Then clambered over the stile.
There I stopped to linger awhile –
I had made another mile.

Finally I followed the path
That ran through the boggy mire.
With squelching steps I made my way,
Back to home by the fire.

So ends a lovely summer's day.
I reflect on an uplifting walk,
Toasting muffins by the fire –
Shame I had nobody with whom to talk.

A ROBIN

I strode along the country path –
It was a summer's day in June,
A clear, blue, cloudless sky –
When I saw a robin in beruffled plume.

I looked up to view the bird,
Perched upon a hawthorn tree.
His little nest was nearby;
He cast a wary eye at me.

The robin has a tiny tail,
And a bright-red breast.
His little wings began to flap –
He's always in his Sunday best.

He flew down to the ground
And landed at my feet.
I knew what he wanted –
He was after a little treat.

And so I duly obliged
With a few seeds.
The robin soon found them,
Scattered in the weeds.

Then I heard some muffled cries
Coming from the nest.
I scattered some extra seeds,
So he could feed the rest.

THE ROWERS

The coxswain barked his racing patter –
There to win was all that mattered.
"If we're going to make another yard,
You'd better pull very hard.
Dip your oars with fettle –
Let us test your mettle.

"You at the bow,
Dig in your oar like a plough."
To the sound of the coxswain's gong,
They rowed their oars deep and long.
The sea lashed the skiff's outer skin;
This did not bother the men within.

The oars were well varnished,
But in the sea they soon tarnished.
The keel was sound and tough.
It did not matter if the sea was very rough –
The skiff slid through the choppy sea
With apparent steady ease.

After a lengthy chase,
The crew came second in the race;
The oarsmen shed a silent tear.
This was the end of the racing year.
They had rowed from the harbour to the pier,
And now gathered in the clubhouse for a welcome beer.

THE SEA

Beneath the briny blue sea,
There's plenty of fishy creatures to see.
On the bottom lies the common crab,
And flatfish like the slippery dab.

In the rocks and weeds
You'll see many a sight indeed –
The scaly ballan wrasse
And the wide-eyed sea bass,

At certain times of day,
The dolphin and porpoise come out to play.
You can see them leap and dive –
It's as though they like to jive.

Other fish in the sea they stay –
The plaice and the large thornback ray,
They live with the Dover sole,
Whose eyes are as black as coal.

The basking shark may emerge from the deep;
At the surface it may rest and sleep,
Basking perfectly still.
With tiny plankton it likes to fill.

The enormous humpback whale
Has an equally large forked tail.
It ducks and dives;
In the deepest water it survives.

Sometimes the pouting
Makes a little outing,
And in the beds of seagrass
A tiny seahorse may slowly pass.

THE SEAHORSE

In the shallows of the blue sea,
In the coastal waters off Torquay,
Lives the seahorse, a tiny creature.
Its resemblance to a horse is its main feature.

Beneath the tide
The seahorse resides.
In the beds of seagrass, a vivid green,
It quietly lives, by man unseen.

It lives on the passing flotsam and jetsam,
Eating the passing morsels, if it can get some.
With the tide the seagrass sways –
In here the seahorse lives its days.

The seahorse lays its eggs in June,
Under the light of a full moon.
When the eggs hatch they will soon grow,
In time their own eggs to sow.

AT THE SEASIDE

The red cliffs hug the wide bay,
And within the breadth of tide's reach,
Where the gulls dance in the sky,
There lies a shifting sandy beach.

Sometimes, in heavy wind and sea,
Foaming white horses grow and ride.
They crash on the shore in mighty waves,
And swell the incoming tide.

There are outcrops of rocks and pools.
In rock pools, sea animals live and breed.
In a dim watery world
They live in the ragwort and weed.

In the sea grass and sand
There are starfish, crab and blenny,
Mussel, cockle and whelk –
Of differing species there are many.

In the rocks, in crooks and crannies,
There lives the delicate prawn.
It feeds on whatever passes by,
And in the shallows it likes to spawn.

Further in the shallower coastal waters
There are shoals of sand eels.
Sand eels are slippery and silver in colour;
They make a snack for the predatory seals.

THE STORYTELLER

The storyteller supped his pint; he had already drunk a few ales,
Now he was ready to tell his tales.
He said, "I like to blether and blellum –
It's not what I say, but the way I tell them."

"Come what may,
I'm here to stay.
I tell ye all,
Je rester ici to the end of the fall.

"We will all live together, cheek by jowl,
To the end of this winter most foul."
They all gathered, grown-ups and bairns,
Plus all the wee wains.

"Now Mary was frae Caithness –
A bonnie lassie, God bless.
She wore a straw bonnet on her crown;
Her hair was long, curly and brown.

"Mary intended wee Davey to woo,
No matter whatever or who.
She said, 'One day he'll be mine,
Even if it takes to the end of time.'

"Now, lads and lassies, listen well,
For I have a few stories to tell.
Be still and let me bend yer ear,
As you drink this wholesome beer.

"Davey was a sergeant in the Black Watch.
He visited his local and liked a Scotch.
He was a good soldier wi' bonnie blue eyes.
'He'll make a good husband,' Mary sighs.

"As for Davey, Mary was a soft spot for him –
He would like to make her his kith and kin.
Soon a romance was in full bloom –
Together they sang many a fine tune.

"Mary lived at the bottom of the glen –
With her mother and father, ye ken.
Their croft was by a babbling burn;
To fetch water they each took a turn.

"As to their future, they didn't dally –
Soon they would tie the knot and marry.
It was to be, they did not falter;
They were joined together at the altar.

"Mary and Davey had two bairns, which they daily kissed.
When in time they flew the nest, they were sorely missed.
The bairns were called Annie and John –
They would soon grow tall and strong.

"When the children left home
They had several kids of their own.
They would have a family get-together
To sing songs and blether.

"Mary was a loving grandmother –
Her grandchildren she liked to smother.
Grandad often took them by the hand –
They played on the beach in the sand."

SPARROWS AND CHAFFINCHES

The sparrows and chaffinches chatter and babble –
Goodness me, they are a noisy rabble.
They sit in the branches and chatter –
They like to have a good natter.

The birds like to have dust baths
In the flower beds beside the paths.
Between them they have lots of chicks to feed,
For whom they constantly search for seed.

The downy chicks slowly get fatter and fatter;
Soon they talk with their parents' patter.
Danger lies in the sparrowhawk, so they post a sentry,
So the hawk cannot gain entry.

SUBURBIA

Detached houses with mock-Tudor facades,
The gardens are always in bloom –
Vibrant water fountains and manicured lawns,
Gardens watered under the light of the moon.

Net curtains and an aspidistra
In the front windows that gleam;
Floor-length velvet curtains;
Dining tables polished to a fine sheen.

Coffee morning at eleven,
The ladies gather for a chat,
Coffee, tea, digestives and cake.
Signs outside: 'Wipe Your Shoes on the Mat'.

Professional men and housebound wives –
The wealthy middle class.
Most can barely afford their bills –
It's all a game, a farce.

Husbands and fathers never at home;
The daily commute to the city.
They hardly see their kids –
So sad, such a pity.

The ladies attend the WI,
They learn arts and craft, making
Endless cups of tea and biscuits,
And they practise home baking.

TORQUAY

Torquay is a lovely place.
Folks sit by the quay eating their fish and chips,
Taking in the sea air,
Watching the boats departing on coastal trips.

In the nearby Debenhams café
A couple enjoy a cream tea
With lashings of jam,
The mother with a child on her knee.

Having finished shopping,
Visitors can leave Torquay town –
A quick drive by car or taxi
Up to peaceful Babbacombe Down.

If they prefer,
They can catch the 'Land Train'
Out to Cockington,
To see the fields of grass and ripe grain.

In Fleet Walk there are lots of stores –
Bonmarché, Shoe Zone, Hoopers and Jane's –
Known by everyone, household names.

In local cafés people can take a break,
Friends and family greet and meet,
Drink tea and coffee,
And rest their aching feet.

From the seafront by the harbour,
Just by the shops,
You can take a ride
On buses with open tops.

Next to the harbour sits Torquay Pavilion –
Sad that it is now an empty shell.
In bygone years, its heyday,
No doubt the walls have a story to tell.

THE DRAGONFLY AND THE TROUT

I sat on the grass, dry and green,
On the banks of the meandering stream,
When something suddenly caught my eye –
A bright dragonfly flew by.

Its body was sparkling blue,
And its wings beat fast as it flew.
It flew low over the water and sometimes skimmed;
Its wings made a humming sound which never dimmed.

The dragonfly was hunting for flies;
For its size it had quite large eyes.
Soon it would shed its larvae under a stone;
For the larvae, this would be their watery home.

I then saw a rainbow trout pop up in the air –
At the dragonfly it did stare.
The trout thought that if it was able,
It would have a fine meal upon its table.

And so began the race –
The hunter and the hunted, a fine chase.
The dragonfly was unaware of the trout's aim;
It did not appreciate the deadly game.

The trout was very adept,
And out of the water it leapt.
However, the dragonfly saw him coming,
And made all the running.

The trout darted in the water below
As it followed the stream's flow.
When it had the opportunity,
It would launch at the dragonfly with impunity.

In the spume and babble of the brook,
The poor dragonfly's life was nearly took.
The trout was keen to have him away,
But the dragonfly lived for many a day.

A TUNA

In Devon, on a cliff path at the headland,
With rucksack and lunch I was walking.
Mist rolled in from the sea below,
And I could hear three men talking.

A man resting on his walking stick,
A fishy story I could hear him tell.
It was a maritime tale,
And he told the story very well.

"The fishing boat headed out to sea,
From Brixham Harbour to Start Bay.
In the deep and choppy waters,
The boat made slow headway.

"The fishermen cast their net;
As they did so, they sang a sailors' song.
The air was damp and salty.
The day's fishing would be very long.

"The capstan hauled in the trawl –
The only catch was one huge tuna fish.
As it was pulled towards the boat,
The crew could see it would make a tasty dish.

"Seagulls circled in the wind overhead;
In the tight net the tuna thrashed.
As they hauled it on to the deck,
Against the side of the boat, the fish bashed.

"The fishermen were skilled,
And had been expertly taught.
For the tuna, it had no idea
It had been trapped and caught.

"The fish was landed on the slippery deck –
It was a small fishing boat;
The tuna nearly stretched from aft to stern.
With good fortune, the vessel stayed afloat.

"The fishing boat then headed for land –
Once again they ploughed the heavy sea.
With a strong east wind behind them,
They would be ashore in time for tea.

"The tuna was taken to Brixham Fish Market –
The tuna is alternatively known as a tunny.
At the auction by the quayside,
The fish was sold for a lot of money."

A SONG THRUSH

On a cold, clear winter's day,
I sat on a park bench and heard a rustle.
It was a female thrush –
With a garden snail it was having a tussle.

The thrush stopped to glance up at me,
To keep out of danger.
I could see its nest nearby,
Hidden in the hydrangea.

The thrush was scavenging in the earth,
Gathering with its beak lots of food.
It then flew into the bush
To feed its hungry brood.

The thrush perched upon a branch.
Its nest is made of twigs and small sticks.
I could hear voices coming from within –
It was a pair of squawking chicks.

WITCHES

On windswept Dartmoor,
In a pine-forest glade,
Various mythical creatures gather
In the shadow of the moon, in the cool shade.

Warlocks and haggard witches
Dance with goblins and Dartmoor pixies –
They reel and jig by the light of a bonfire.
Dressed like a warlock, the local town crier.

They dance the Highland fling,
Swirl as they move, clap and sing,
On the cold autumnal night.
Auld Nick looks on – the black towzy tyke.

With horses and ponies tethered,
The folks chatted and blethered.
For firewood, they had gathered a lot –
This kept the flames piping hot.

THE WREN

The wren's plumage is barred and brown,
Its breast is velvet-soft down.
The wren, it likes to preen,
To keep its feathers nice and clean.

The wren forages in the grass and sedge,
And sometimes perches upon my window ledge.
In the birdbath it takes a sip;
Sometimes it takes a little dip.

It moves on the lawn to seek
Moss to gather with its beak.
With this it builds a mossy nest –
It works constantly without a rest.

Wrens mainly live alone,
But sometimes bring a partner home.
They will duly mate –
Baby chicks they will create.

Spiders and insects are their main diet;
They feed the chicks to keep them quiet.
The chicks grow in the nest within –
They make quite a merry din.